(ΦMALE)
(PHIMALE)

FEMALE BODY RETOLD

Giorgia Pavlidou

*Countercharming Matt Walsh's
Black Magic Question:
'What Is A Woman?'*

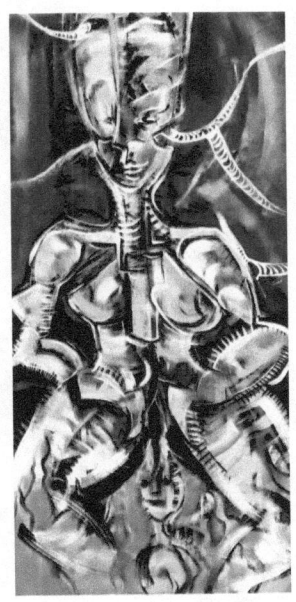

SPUYTEN DUYVIL
New York City

"Meanwhile, feminists regularly insist that the absence of a uterus and a vagina excludes men from having an opinion about things like abortion. So, a man can't have ideas about women's issues because he lacks the correct anatomy, but he can actually be a woman despite lacking the correct anatomy? How does that make any kind of sense?"

Matt Walsh

Cyborg: "a fictional or hypothetical person whose physical abilities are extended beyond normal human limitations by mechanical elements built into the body."

"Cycladic culture was a bronze age culture (c.3100—c. 1000 BC) found throughout the islands of the Cyclades in the Aegean Sea."

Contents

To begin with:

March 2023

At a café in downtown Athens, Greece,
while writing a letter to William Blake,
a bizarre potpourri of sounds apprehended me:

drilling,
sad 1980 new wave tunes,
caged canaries' manic chirping,
early spring's sunbeams
crackling through winter's last legs' convulsions,

seagulls' high-pitched screeching.

Regarding the latter I asked myself:

"What news are these sonic sky rats bringing me from the
extreme outer edges of discordance?"

INTRODUCTION

WHERE CONSCIOUSNESS CANNOT GO

"Poetry brings all possible experience to the same degree:
a degree in consciousness beyond which
consciousness itself cannot go."
–Laura Riding

John Olson:

Language severs us from reality. It's also what prods and aids us to explore the nature of reality. The reality of reality. Language forgets it has a body. Language forgets it lives in a body. Language forgets it is produced by a body. Tongue, palate, larynx, glottis, trachea, nasal cavity. To name a few. The driving force of the poetry in this book is to make these issues explicit with the candy of anarchy. The candor and incandescence of anarchy. Why anarchy? The anarchic spirit is the electricity that lights our thoughts and warms our beds. Its pertinence to poetry should be obvious. Its pertinence (and/or impertinence) to this particular collection is charged with conflicts of sexuality and female identity, a "circle of pain" Pavlidou illumines with colorful phrases like "the myriad odors of the abnormal," "the perfume of perversion," and "the potassium of agony eats us up." Syllables of lyrical beauty in a goo of hungry protein, "poisonous as well as therapeutic / both dead and alive / male and female at once." Human sexuality is a very difficult dance, whether one is binary, duplex, or double-barreled. At base, we're what Pavlidou calls "φonemic bodies," creatures of language with "lexical tentacles." It's a peculiar thought, a maddening paradox, to find such jouissance amid so much violence. All this to say that this collection is an intense, highly unique approach to poetry I don't recall seeing anywhere else. A bit sci-fi, yet very Greek, Pythian, Delphic, oracular. A lot of sass to it, too.

Roberta Olson:

"Woman is an invention, a social construct" ~ Thaddeus Russell
Are humans post-biology? Should we be? What is the purpose of gender? Is gender identification with various traits and societal patterns or is gender merely biological? Biologically gender is a means to reproduction. Giorgia Pavlidou states in her long poem "Female Body Retold,"

> "This is a thoughtless world
> Drip drop drip drop drip drop drip drop and next:
> A downpour of eternity …"

The world as being. Ephemeral existence. Being is more than reproduction, the "downpour of eternity" lies in an impossible sameness. Last autumn, I took two cuttings from a fuchsia plant before a killing frost. I rooted them indoors under a grow-light and they grew through the winter far exceeding my expectations. Although they were born of the same stem, they were individuals. One had two stems and was lush, the other had one stem and had a tree-like quality. Their individuation created my attachment to them, created a sense of loss because of their uniqueness. Their differences gave them narrative. We have words to articulate our world but words themselves are inscrutable. Pavlidou states this aptly:

> "The word is a verdant Spirit being
> The word is all creativity
> Yet shrewd"

How far we have gone from nature with our language, our questioning. The book has a writhing feel. An arduous twisting out of our painful consciousness. Slippery identity dream states madness. *Female Body Retold* leads us through the underworld of the word in a quest for the uniquely human need for identity.

John:

This is true. Consciousness hurts. What are we doing with it? Why is it here? If everything is molecular, what separates the organic from the inorganic? What are categories for? What are taxonomies for? They're useful for social organization and marketing things. But they don't explain the permeability of boundaries, the exchange of fluids between capillaries and tissues, the osmotic imbroglio between friends and enemies, or how an image like "the dripping sound of thought" can transit so quickly from abstraction to palpable occurrence. I love those lines, too.

Pavlidou is a sorceress of the ineffable, and the agonistic. How did you put it? "The book has a writhing feel. An arduous twisting out of painful consciousness." It's a book with an attitude. It has issues. Bones to pick. "She quotes several controversial figures such as Matt Walsh (who calls himself a "theocratic fascist"), and Jordan Peterson, whose presence here has a leaden weight.

You've got to wonder why academics like Jordan Peterson (who Pavlidou quotes as antagonist rather than ally) get so exercised over the issue of pronouns, but especially postmodernism. It's just an ism, not a monster. Why take it that seriously? It's not doctrine. It's provocation. It's quantum. It's non-linear. It reflects the discoveries of particle accelerators, new insights into the nature of energy and matter. Heisenberg's Uncertainty Principle. The God Particle.

People love that Whitman quote about contradiction, "Very well then, I contradict myself, I am large, I contain multitudes." Sounds like a succinct example of postmodernism to me. Does that make it terrible? Does it cause people to become lost and ignorant? Does it promote boorishness? Callowness? Gullibility? Authoritarianism? It seems to me to do the very opposite of that.

Manicheaism is for dark worlds of chaos, brutality and dogma. This makes Pavlidou's play with polarities all the more interesting. She loves paradox: "i'm exiting / stepping as slow as i can / into an outside that's also an inside." Her use of conundrum and riddle to support the themes of this collection play out in ways that emphasize the nomadic movements of consciousness.

If I can imagine a fire, why can't I also feel a fire? And if I feel a fire is the fire in some way speaking to me? The older I get the more hylozoistic I become: why else did I feel so sad when our Subaru was towed away. All matter is charged with life. Categories can ruin everything. Male, female. Organic, inorganic. Categories are procrustean. They pinch like lotus shoes.

Pavlidou is a very physical poet. The sensuous dynamic of physicality is everywhere in this work, as forcefully present as the story in the bible about Jacob wrestling God. The link between physicality and the way we embody language, or language embodies us, is a daily preoccupation.

I like the way symphony conductors communicate music with their bodies. It looks a little like dance, but it's not dance. It's something else. The movements can be herky-jerky or slow and graceful, but there's always a clear intent to these gestures, it's clear the conductor is telegraphing information about tone and timbre, rhythm and melody, the shape of the music, the way it breathes, the way it brings something crucial and visceral to the arena of human emotion and puts that energy into the bow going across a set of strings or the breath channeled through an oboe. This tells me the connection between language and body might be even stranger than we think. Maybe it was language that brought us into being. Or maybe it's still trying to bring us into being.

Roberta:

Did language bring us into being? Pavlidou begins the poem "the alchemy of ambiguity" with Ἐν ἀρχῇ ἦν ὁ λόγος, καὶ ὁ λόγος ἦν πρὸς τὸν θεόν, καὶ θεὸς ἦν ὁ λόγος, the first lines of John 1:1, which in English translates as: "In the beginning was the Word and the Word was with God and the Word was God." An echo of our creation story from Genesis 1:1 "In the beginning was heaven and earth..." I may be overly analytical but further on in Genesis there is a repetition of what God SAID before creating the world. "And God said let there be light and there was light." If you think about it, language has always defined our world and being. We cannot escape taxonomy and it can be useful in nature. If you can name something you know how to approach it, how to care for it; but humans seem to be something post-natural. Natural definitions do not quite reach us. Is there a distinction between the word woman and female? Female is a taxonomy. In nature the female is the one who receives and the one who brings forth. Woman describes the human female, but it is rife with societal baggage carried by the female purpose in nature. Woman the nurturer, woman the passive, woman the sensitive. The problem is when society applies labels like cages and locks the door.

The circle of pain comes up a lot in "The Female Body Retold." Throughout the book there are spinning, whirling sacred dances and chaotic revelry. Always spinning. The way we circle meaning, the way our minds spin seeking identity:

"I am the center of a circle of pain/ Exceeding its boundaries in every direction"

"Red dervishes' whirl upside down, / under a naked turquoise lake, /swirling letters curly and suspended still on the horizon."

"Contours of whirling silhouettes/ Wearing long skirts/ Circle in high velocity through thick mist"

"Movements drip and spur dark acrylic paint"

Later in the poem we encounter the very real and unique human struggle with identity again swirling around us:

"I've seen sacred drag-queens whirl in ecstasy/ Appearing as hyper-feminine druids/ with balls."

The human condition as question. We are the beings who create our own place in the world. For better or worse. Our consciousness seems primed to question our place in the world. Who we are what we must do. At first, I saw this as a type of vanity but now thanks to my reading and thinking about Giorgia Pavlidou's "Female Body Retold" I realize that this question is both the burden and the grace of being human. Maybe we could give ourselves and others enough space for our own individual quests.

John:
I would like to add two short quotes about language by the linguist Edward Sapir that go to the heart of what is under discussion here: "Language is the most massive and inclusive art we know, a mountainous and anonymous work of unconscious generations…," which would, of course, extend back to the time when Genesis was first composed, and "What fetters the mind and benumbs the spirit is ever the dogged acceptance of absolutes," which supports Roberta's statement about language as a form of social governance, applying labels like cages and locking the door, i.e. accepting a semantic representation as absolute truth. This focus on those beautiful passages of genesis in the bible and the way they exalt language to such an omnipotent scale provides a framework for poetic development in a mortar and pestle trituration of contraries.

"To extend your life," Pavlidou counsels, "you first must become sick. Take / my medicine…My illness will keep you healthy. You must eat the horizon." These lines are from "Intergalactic Pharmacist" in the section that introduces Cycladic Cyborg. Why Cyborg?

A cyborg is a being with both organic and biomechatronic body parts. Arnold Schwarzenegger in *Terminator*. Pris in *Blade Runner*. The Buffybot in *Buffy the Vampire Slayer*. Beings embodying state control and/or technocratic evangelism. Humanoids bearing the brunt of technological arrogance, like Rutger Hauer's "replicant" in *Blade Runner*, and his dying lines: "I've seen things you people wouldn't believe. Attack ships on fire off the shoulder of Orion. I watched C-beams glitter in the dark near the Tannhäuser Gate. All those moments will be lost in time, like tears in rain." The idea embedded in this drama is that the cyborg is at once more highly empowered than mortal human beings, but cruelly limited to a four-year life span. Language simultaneously empowers and limits, and is both a curse and a blessing.

One of the more salient features stylistically empowering Pavlidou's poesis of conflict and triumph over the kind of reductive, linguistic categories language sinks into when it gets monotonous and tired and the citizenry lose their focus and begin, out of anxiety and mental laziness, to call for censorship and restrictions in order to control the monster, is to fragment the language in scintillas of ecstasy and delirium, both undermining devices of patriarchal control and creating agencies of orgasmic release. There's the risk of obscurantism and slipping into a fug of aestheticized and solipsistic impotence, but this is avoided by sheer outrageousness, the acetylene torch of a maenad in the poetic arena, welding metonym to Sprechstimme, metaphor to hellebore. It's a hedonistic polemic of fusion and synthesis, mutation, and disputation.

ROBERTA & JOHN OLSON. SEATTLE, APRIL 2023

S-1 : Φ

THE ΦONEMIC BODY

"tu es etiam socia angelorum et civis sanctorum"
Hildegard Von Bingen

INTERGALACTIC PHARMACIST : क

Eat this preamble:

While hidden in sound,
Cycladic cyborg addresses *pauper creatura femina*,
the uber-suggestable Sophia Diamantidou,

zealous collector of hallucinations
& psychosomatic symptoms.

i

No central heating this winter, only a hissing wood stove in Sophia's
hollow little chamber.

Flames hadn't broken through yet.

Dry twigs were still going *shshshshshshshshsh,* when one of its decibels
amplified into a whisper, saying:

"Sophia, I'm the only on-duty intergalactic pharmacist.
I sell medicine to the healthy. One million years ago,
I sold an extraordinary product to your planet.
You hearing this proves my medicine works.

First you were healthy but died fast.
Now you're sick but live quite long."

ii
Red dervishes' whirl upside down,
under a naked turquoise lake,
swirling letters curly
& suspended still on the horizon.

There the letters sparkle & say:

"To extend your life,
you first must become sick.
Take my medicine.
Swallow once daily
& triple your years.

My illness will you keep healthy.
You must eat the horizon."

***

Cycladic cyborg continues her whispers. She introduces new
characters: Canadian psychologist & YouTube Personality, Jordan
Peterson,
Zuni princess We'Wha & a few others. Sophia eats them all.

***

iii
Ho ho ho,

here gallops Viking Peterson,
zealous collector of truth & other autoimmune disorders, stuttering
Jungian facts on Youtube,
he bears sparkling little gifts for the First Sex.

& who we have here?

We'Wha,
mid-19th century Zuni princess:
she needed neither bones nor genitals,
for D.C. to celebrate her womanhood.

What about that, Santa Peterson?
Your anthropological facts got you banned from Twitter.

Intergalactic pharmacist becomes Eliot Page.
On TikTok, Eliot's avatar says:

"To become binary,
you first must become many.
Take my medicine.
Swallow twice daily
& quadruple your sex.

My groin will keep you divided.
You must eat Twitter."

iv
Contours of whirling silhouettes
wearing long skirts,
circle in high velocity
through thick mist.

Movements drip
& spur dark acrylic paint
splashing lyrical letters
floating uphill,

saying:

"Imagine there's no woman.
On planet Winter, there's no gender.
Ursula's *Gethenians* can become male or female during each
mating cycle,
& this is something
Matt Walsh finds indigestible.

Walsh must eat a *Gethian*."

v

Sophia whirls & swings in seven dance passes, that barge into a
head, that twist from the edge of thought,

that cough up a mind.

Seven poems without center collapse into the myriad aromas of
the abnormal.

Savor here the perfume of perversion:

"I am the center
of a circle of pain
exceeding its boundaries
in every direction."

Eleven colors
Five Vowels

Hear, hear,
the brimming textures of the anti-life

Hope,
a banana peeled from the inside out

Near stony places,
the potassium of agony eats us up.

Birthed by the machinery of infinity,
Sophia's thoughts paint:

"Listen to the dripping sound of thought.
This is a thoughtless world:
Drip drop drip drop drip drop drip drop,
& next:

a downpour of eternity."

Infinity condensed into eleven vowels

Third is also here,
the double

Two in one person
Witness the birth of the *di-vidual*; Sophia chews on an individual,

until the *Blue-Throated One* chants:

girly turquoise face glistered with gusto for shenanigans:

she sat
giggling inside an   endless   vowel; heee heee-hiding &
whispering to Sophia:

hear here the story of my creation:

THE ANNUNCIATION : ख

i
once
i was like you:

a white protein bag
a wrinkled sack of bowels and bones

a machine
manufacturing miniature machines every nine months

i was wife daughter mother

though in nightdreams
naked cyborgs sang to me

faceless females undulating as if gigantic transparent snakes

violent arrhyθmic beats flooded my earshot

                              fire *crackled-crackled-crackled*

in the center of this dark chaos
the prima *materia* of human flesh & plastic

my own corpse appeared ablaze
on an operating theater

a young woman's body enclosed by θroat singing trolls chanting in
polyphonic overtones

while medical robots rewrote my skin

while white coats re-spun my nervous system

ii
my eyelids cracked open
the morning after

when words trembled wriggled
swum
under my skin

glossolalic fishtails waved inside my womb
pisces with decibels for scales
fluttered their invisible fins

organs whispered

murmurs-murmurs-murmurs

of an alien syntax

shrieking sounds as if resurrected from languages long gone extinct

annunciating that:

on the first day of the 6th month after march 25th

the day bodies of θought burned up

Ὄσιρις,

serpents squirmed θrough rivers of asphalt
& uttered:

"et ecce concipies in utero

ohne dich kann ich nicht leben."

iii
once i was human, parents and grandparents raised me

brothers & sisters loved & hated me

i birthed a baby boy i detested & adored

alas,
on the 6th month
my genitals
imploded into a meltdown
of ecstatic sighs

my organs had turned plastic
my mind electric
my skin appeared synθetic
my womb φonemic

stroke my silicone nipples
kiss my plastic lips
be perplexed by my lexical fluidity

on the 9th month when
i entered labor

    celestial triangles penetrated circles, circles caressed squares,
        the letter φ kissed the letter χῖ,
        water was seduced to disrupt,
        fig trees peeled
        & devoured their own fruit

iv
my births can never be reduced to one or two
nor my punctuation,

this silicone body gestates pluralities
multi-polar embryos
gifted with perpetual regeneration

painted specters
in constant φonemic expansion

& my adjectives, look:

they're watching sonic winds!
lingual hailstorms in black holes

intergalactic φonemes

                    knock-knock-knock

against a relentless human skull

iv
this ⲫonemic body was announced by the oblique
its lexical tentacles burrowed in human skin

observe zillions of swarming infixes spiraling up my spine

undulating around my neurotransmitters, undulating around my phonemes

this ⲫonemic body/this synthetic body/this one true body

evaporates
when one tries looking into all its eyes

eight-eight-eight

plastic tongues
whispered sweet words

perhaps three times
perhaps seven times

& billions of splendiferous voices sprouted in my head

singing songs from the future
songs of experience
songs stripped of all
consonants

songs of innocence

excommunicated

eternally

from
their
native tongues

"You can lie to yourself all you want, but you cannot drag me into it. And so it goes for pronouns. If I intentionally call a man "she," I have lied. I have conveyed something that isn't true. Despite my polite intentions, all I've done is contribute to the confusion, dishonesty, and intellectual chaos rampant in our culture."
—Matt Walsh

"The Gethenians do not see one another as men or women."
—Ursula K. Le Guin, The Left Hand of Darkness

"Pygmies are being pursued in the forests. People have been eaten."
—Sinafi Makelo

WE'WHA's JOURNEY TO D.C. : ग

i
Encroached by seas of infertility,
with tides annunciating post-mortem comings:

your two-folded Zuni current
sparkled through drabness.

Two-in-One,
Third-yet-Zero,
Yes & No
condensed into
Neither & Both,

meet the speaking red-rusting landscapes
that resisted the ambush of new speech:

"the great Anti-Castrators of the Unimaginable."

ii
fiber artist
weaver
potter
hailed as Zuni Princess in D.C.
called "the most intelligent person of the Pueblo"

You spun baffling phonologies
You planted confusion in Mathilda Stevenson's binary mind

trampled on alien thought
by tiptoeing through foreign syntax

your tripolar being
pulverized imported rationalities

like Sophia,
you united the already joined
separated the never disjointed
you never were optical illusion
your Being merely exposed
accusatory mirages:

what is a Woman?
what is a Pygmy?

Gaining entrance into personhood has never been *gratis*.
Tolls are always levied with unequal *Calliope*

iii
& thus the delegation left New Mexico
crossed an ancient territory deemed brand-new, baptized after an
exogenous cartographer, voyaging to the capital of a foreign country
declared & settled on your ancestral land

this,
We'wha, constituted your triangular experiments

& Sophia whispers:

"to become binary,
you first must become at least three.
swallow my medicine,
& cut yourself in half.
your division will keep you united."

referred as 'he,' later as 'she,'
Stevenson eventually settled on 'she.'

Eat that Matt
eat her height
eat her bones
eat her genitals

& Sophia,
lonely as a fish
even in new American light
even in Rochelle Owens' presence
even in Mina Loy's ever-exceeding circles of pain

Pauper Creatura Femina,
zealous collector of visions,

Osteopath of Language,

as lonely as Hildegard
as lonely as the poet
as lonely as those who speak borrowed tongues, as lonely as those
who refuse to accept the instant contours of the barely imaginable:

Matt Welsh must eat a *Gethian*

iv
Cycladic cyborg
whirls from the edge of embodiment
over Jordan Peterson's galloping
into reversed silicone impossibilities:

"& bewildering lights tickle into Polar Delights,
& bewildering Nights seep into red-whirling endless Nights."

these,
are the nocturnal destinies of the glacial

these,
are the synthetic annunciations of the one true body,

these,
splash up Sophia's black acrylic thoughts:

listen to the dripping sound of thought.
this is a thoughtless world:
drip drop drip drop drip drop drip drop, & next,
a downpour of Eternity:
Infinity condensed into eleven vowels.

Third is also here
the Double
Two in one person

witness the birth of the *di-vidual*, Sophia chews on an individual,
till the *Blue-Throated One* stated:

"Enter here the Black Hornet's Mind-Tunnel"

THE BLACK HORNET'S MIND-TUNNEL : घ

i
& as for राक्षसी
 or अपसरस
fluttering inside celestial black insects

&
as for महाकाली

her name milked from the same
word as Time & Black

she disguises herself as the tiny
but inevitable daily death

what is it she's taking with her,
vibrating black kleptoparasite?

you know best

because it is *you*

who's the undertaker of the mind

the light of your language
liberates

cremate my brain
if you must

you osteopath of spirit

manipulate my meandering mind
if you will

&

i'll eat
bursts of

your

carnivorous syntax

ii
& because
i'm reflecting on your electromagnetic sting
as charged with the voltage of manic wasp medicine

i consider your telekinetic Φ*armakon*
a form of extraterrestrial mutation

harvested from multiple dimensions
it is:
poisonous as well as therapeutic
both dead and alive male and female at once

it is your धर्म i'm talking about

the law of right action
sizzling
beyond the noon-tide of the dead

remember,
there are fictive realities
tucked deep inside the real of your illusions

these pulverize intrusive thoughts

& as you've shown with artaud and van gogh you excel in

transforming
schizophrenia into the arts of life

iii
beloved insect
your tentacles control psychosis

as if swarms of
spectral phantoms
faint like a poem without a center
when you watch them in the eyes
eight-eight-eight

your exobiology
defies drabness

your vibrations are fluid
liquid

never obvious
never sullen

the light of your language
is relentless

you are fire dressed in fire

iv
around the magnetism of your fangs
the depressed
before recovery
first loose their minds

in your presence suicidal thoughts obliterate calcinate
decompose or turn into rubber &
look at your black exoskeleton

written with the blinding brightness of your language:

being lava clothed in lava
you fight fire with fire
let *me*
fight
psychosis with psychosis

v

we've arrived at the final act:

in this instant with your help,
kali's inorganic biology is birthing myriads of minds

& in exchange for your homeopathic spores:

she promises to protect you

forever

                                        once you're inside her

                            inside the black hornet's mind-tunnel

राक्षसी
guarantees you you'll as be as safe as infinity
sculpted
inside a mummy

safe
as if
forever
embalmed into
a memory

safe
as long
as eternity
&
a millisecond, i promise you

PYTHIA COUNSELS TS ELIOT'S GHOST : ड़

i
Meet the tender scavengers of ontology, traffickers in hidden scripts,
dredging up from the edge of

perversion,

ritual dramas of hallucination,
in which

intergalactic pharmacist enacts:

"Possum Eliot,
while writing
you cultivated parasites in your brain, &
your symptoms simmered under the skin

Things did not fall apart,
as your buddy William suggested.

You discovered how 'cobalt imposters,
as annihilative raconteurs,
always operate in secret.'

The postmodern dead, Possum,
refuse to be buried.

Nowadays,
the pre-mortem crave cremation.

'Like cats or snakes,'
euthanasia
is what the barely-living desire.

'The cocksuckers, TS Eliot, the cocksuckers.
Muddy with tears
meat for the whip
Tooth or boot for the cowgirls.'"

ii
American half-objects swing
tenderly
with white acrylic paint

&
splash
affectionately,
inherently unanswerable questions on twitter:

"Worlds without dualisms: do they exist?
Worlds without antagonists: do they exist?

Envision a carnivorous America with only democrats.
Envision a vegetarian America with only republicans:

How would such a world look like?

Hildegard, while bedridden in Eibingen Abbey, wonders:

Quid hoc mundo simile?
Wie sahe so eine welt aus?

& in Delphi
Mina Loy speaks through Pythia:

   rocks of human mist nylon jazz gas doorways   Zyklon-B portals petals

once again,
the petals of the unsayable are about to flower up

once again,
the plastic petals of the unsayable have flowered up

once again,
the gas portals to enhanced cognition refuse to close down

this,
is thoroughly thoughtless world:

Drip drop drip drop drip drop drip drop,
& next:

a downpour of eternity.

Thought condensed into eleven vowels

We're cremating cognition, Possum
Immediately & affectionately

chew
eternally
on the indefinite
affectionate
yet disastrous decibels of the unsayable:

in postmodernity, Eliot

as you couldn't have known,

the dying live eternities
& the living yearn to die

iii
these plastic symptoms secured the neglected business of negative
embodiment

the day after yesterday   which isn't today today is the double:
two-in-one-yet-zero

none of the other bodies went bankrupt,
the technobodies

&
in Delphi
Pythia's business of speaking in tongues counsels,

Immediately & affectionately:

"don't
die a premature death   abolish slavery instead
by turning everyone into a slave: ha!"

I
am a sexy sociopath,

You
a sexy slavedriver

Sophia knows both cotton fields & workplaces are the tender receptacles of black magic.

Dearest pederasts,
I'm advising you,
homosexual techno-sapiens
equal a myriad of moral dilemmas,
but through Matt's film
morality will destroy & salvage us all

Immediately & affectionately

In Matt's marvelous movie,
the plastic sellers of coherence will fruitlessly try & castrate
the myriad perfumes of perversion

rub
while you still can
on your silicone skin   & in slow motion   the amphibian
ointments of arousal:

Anal sex,
Chicks with dicks,
"Meat for the whip
Toot or booth for the cowgirls."

"Come, words, away from mouths,
Away from tongues in mouths
And reckless hearts in tongues
And mouths in cautious heads—

Come, words, away to where
The meaning is not thickened
With the voice's fretting substance,
Nor look of words is curious
As letters in books staring out
All that man ever thought strange
And laid to sleep on white
Like the archaic manuscript
Of dreams at morning blacked on wonder."
                    —Laura Riding

AVASCULAR VISHNU : च

when once below a time you blurred up
deep past & far future by deliberate accident

you obliterated
neat delineations of succession

in spaces where one is forced to dwell in Χρόνος
as in महाकाल moving in all directions at the same time
as in living-breathing
Θάνατος

not as in cheap science fiction
nor as in infantile back-to-the-future
but as in yesterday-and-tomorrow-at-once

as in two-in-one-yet-zero
liberated from diachrony
        there
on transparent territories of synchrony
in between the celestial cogs of eternity, at the extreme outer
edges of linearity

one million oracles whirl to fuse with your dharma:
these are the laborers of thought

you,
neither mechanic nor organic
neither yin nor yang

ostracized from
yet never sentenced, nor to duality neither to opposition

you are completely at home in domains devoid of desire & contrast

you're an anarchist of perception
creator & slayer of seasonality   perpetually perpetuating perpetuity

as non-stop thirdness
as existence
& non-existence in continuous copulation

in this boundless region of eternal renewal

one meets You:
Vishnu devoid of vascularity

frequencies of your dharma
flutter in all carbon-based experiencing

& let's take Laura
who with her Fugitives unknowingly tried courting you

she rode to find you in between soundwaves

Laura Reichenthal
who tried spinning non-linguistic truths, who tried hiding in silence
who tried escaping the diachronous

shepherdess of vocabulary, as she was huntress of grammar
she tried escaping into the ontic but failed

perhaps there's no silence, Vishnu of the Vatic
hence this failure & non-being
as eternal

circling back continuously
You Avascular Vishnu

As Cycladic
As post-human
As dusk & dawn at once
where humanity & divinity overlap

In the vast amount of voices we can't escape hearing
In background muttering we must dwell

In which
Cycladic cyborg
cyclically returns to the center of Aegean

The intergalactic pharmacist
Planter of voices in heads of the uber-suggestible
Sonic medicine

In heads like Sophia Diamantidou's
Pauper creatura femina
Bedridden in Los Angeles
Reading Rochelle Owens poetry out loud
Feeling even more lonely than a fish

Lonely as the poet-philosopher
Lonely as the poet-exorcist

Even in New American Light
Even in Mina Loy's ever exceeding circles of pain
Even when We'wha was hailed as a Zuni princess in D.C.

You circled back, avascular Vishnu
To whisper in the ontic scavengers' ears

Ramping up Pythia's business of speaking in tongues
Immediately & Affectionally

The following inconclusive words:

"Sophia, this medicine you've been swallowing
is inaccurate yet adequate.

Continue this linguistic treatment,
& you'll be spared the turbulent arena of the accurate.

We're in dire need of theocratic fascists like Matt Walsh.

It's only through opposition that
crafting Being becomes possible.
From New Mexico to D.C.,
from Eibingen Abbey to Hampstead,
from the center of the Aegean to Brooklyn,
from Istanbul to Banaras,
from Ituri Forest in Northern Congo to Mumbai:

these are the nocturnal destinies of the glacial.

"Muddy with tears,
meat for the whip,
tooth of boot for the cowgirls:"

Wie sahe so eine welt aus?

Possum,
One million years ago,
Cycladic Cyborg sold an extraordinary
product to your ancestors.

You hearing this,
proves her medicine works.

First you were healthy but died fast.
Now you're sick but live quite long."

S-2 : θ

THE ALCHEMY
OF AMBIGUITY

The Wicked have injured the Earth
Poets know all about it
Only Poets can save the Earth
from Extinction

—Namdeo Dhasal

"Poetry is not conventional social literature. It is the discovery of the materiality of consciousness, whether in the sound of a car starting, the tension of a shoulder muscle, or the floating of an owl feather in a breeze."

—Michael McClure

SEXLESS HALF-OBJECTS

slow   deliberate movements

absences of trembling

as intentional as yesterday's arthouse movie

two hands in frozen refusal of quivering

they open an unlocked door   in-slow-motion

as calculating as a yesterday

 i'm exiting stepping as slow as i
can

into an outside that's also an inside

deeper into this hazy be-sides

the apparition of a small family of adorable
but sexless half-objects waves at me

my hands refuse all waving
yet i wave i wave i wave.

A Vampire Called Eurydice

How comfortable the warm darkness of caskets --
Doubtlessly finer than nowadays' low-quality blood

Still much to my surprise,
Orpheus eventually arrived. I followed his back for a little while, bumping
against a shadow or two   (more to stay true to the myth instead of really
wanting to)

Yet I was curious: "Will he succeed this time around?"

As was to be expected, he turned his head once again --
Tired, stuffy, dark circled eyes looked at me for the umpteenth time.
He didn't impress me much; I feel forced to confess.
Or was he a she? Or a they? Difficult to say, today:

Even genitals have minds of their own -- on this present day.

Relieved my hero had so blatantly failed once more,
I returned to the comforting darkness of my sepulcher
(*apropos:* my relationship with light has never been exceptionally bright).

Hades isn't such a bad place after all, I thought, while my coffin welcomed
me back inside.

The embittered Goddess, Persephone, stared at me with her usual pitch-
black eyes.

I drooled gazing back at her magnificent, mean, pale, perforating face.
And before I could even think of rising up, and lick her insipid dark lips,
her hungry tongue, deep inside my menial and brittle little mouth,
was already done circling around mine:

So-so comfortable – something mandated me to think - *the convivial darkness of my casket.*

Much-much more exquisite and finer than nowadays' low-quality blood.

Een duivel raast voorbij:
Taste here the speed of hir desire

METAPHYSICS OF A PINK BEDROOM

an ambitious girl
from macedonia
i think

trained in germany
to maneuver herself
in every pornographic
position imaginable

ex-researcher
of pierre bourdieu at the sorbonne

familiar as well
with whitman & ginsberg

reserved for a balkan lady
i thought
even when drunk on guinness

something happened
she said
before she'd grown pubic hair:
a mixture of noir-folklore & illegal porn

she looked 36
this recently grown-up balkan chick
the age she'd reach in 16 years

36's very old
she said

but who doesn't fear old age
when it keeps on
kicking in your childhood's door

i pondered
on how five billion years were needed
for the solar system to produce her story
& for both of us to squirm in a molded bed
incapable of escaping reality's fungus:

experiencing the uncanny metaphysics of a pink bedroom

perhaps it's common in macedonia
i mused inside my head
this talent for french sociology
& these gratis tears rolling down one's cheeks

elliptical drops
resembling disfigured circles around the sun:
as elliptical & incomprehensible as french theory

with copies
of her words echoing in all important airports of the european union

slavonic breathing
while it seemed as if it would never stop raining outside

sighs
waiting near a pile of over-stuffed working-class garbage bags

harboring
a few mute body-parts
& a smiling unloaded gun

plus
the obese excrements
of mid-21st century urban rats

impossible to redeem oneself
even when flagellating oneself
i thought

& i admired her face:
a weeping nation of deeply stunning scars

an innocence so blinding
capable of setting one's gaze on fire

a human pile of unwelcomed love on a severely guillotined bed

& that

without reality's agony at hand
to run towards & escape into

meet here:
two sorrowful & lonely orgasms
lingering on a reality-infested bed

not truly like hurricanes
but pointless like unused body parts
or loudly laughing unloaded guns

many elliptical heads
must have rolled
from this guillotined bed
she said

invisible only to those who have succeeded
in failing to avoid loving someone else

despite
having <u>plenty</u> of
reality's agony
at hand
to run towards
& escape into

i thought
but abstained

from saying back

AN UNSARCASTICALLY SMILING SKY

Time's dissolving me
in front of an unsarcastically smiling sky

Hollow trees roll their eyes
Missing cobblestones laugh at my future non-existence

"It's there where you're headed,"
a voice in my head whispers,
"towards your absence."

"Come all,
drink from the fountain of my non-being," the voice makes me
say out loud.

But none of the random passersby
moves in my direction

"I believe in all religions."
—John Coltrane

"I pestled my heart in love's mortar, roasted it & ate it."
—Lalla

WHY ON 8TH STREET?
for philip lamantia

i
contemplating my poetry ancestors
not Sappho,

but   hildegard von bingen & lalla   came to mind

& unexpectedly

these two cojoined   conjured up saint coltrane's image:

a siamese triplet bound by the blinding intensity of the living light

listen in a uniquely visual way   to the sound of this light
turn inward & hear mandalas meander

on *pineappled* boundaries of the pre-sexed brain:
this - is - hildegard's - syntax:

"tu es etiam socia angelorum et civis sanctorum"

(you are indeed the companion of the angels & a citizen of holiness)

enormous transparent lakes filled with whirling black dolphins
                              stay
  suspended high up

                                        in turquoise summer sky

iii
my mind boomed with this view   & half-notes grilled my body
via 3rd & 7th street i was guided to 8th street

"philip, on 8th street
my body reentered the uterine source of life"

it's - there – where - you'll – find - hildegard's - syntax:

  "caritas habundat in omnia, se imis excellentissima super sidera"
              (love abounds in all, from the depths exalted
                    and excelling over every star)

GROWING OLD IN AMERICA AS A WOMAN
SEEMS UNREASONABLY EXCITING

First, I bicker with the stubborn hairs running up my female face. Luckily, my mustache, the cleverest of cognitive sheep dogs, herds them into two rectangular packs. Very geometric of him. Next, a demanding but unreasonably smiling mirror laughs loudly at my flocks of missing teeth. If I hadn't earlier peeled the rare smile off my face, I wouldn't be able to observe the grazing thoughts flocking to my rural grin. At times, two or three patriotic sheep get stuck in between my gorge-like wrinkles.

One scruffy-looking goat, being as mulish as a thought-cowboy, hides behind two massive warts. There's an unusually thick hair growing on top of the most mountainous mole of all. Its reflection smiles at me as well, unsarcastically of course. A masculine-looking banner seems attached to this hair. The flag flutters gayly. At last, I'm seeing a smile reappear on my barely female face when the words, "growing old as a woman in America seems unreasonably exciting," unexpectedly pop up in my head.

COSMIC CYCLOPS

What would happen if an angel appeared among us?
Sold as a slave?
Shred to pieces?
Dissected?
Extracted to be used as an aphrodisiac?
Crucified?

No inter-dimensional being would ever dare coming to our world, I think
Extraterrestrial beings probably wouldn't even consider traveling to the
blue planet
They're not crazy
They're not suicidal
Unless, of course, they're giants

& why wouldn't they be giants
Our star is a dwarf
Our planet is tiny

Intergalactic Cyclops are brewing plans, perhaps
But what could they possibly gain from coming over?
Surely they wouldn't travel light years to have us as a snack
Perhaps *en route* to somewhere else?

They might land on Earth as a stopover
Like picking up a breakfast burrito, while
Driving to the office
Imagine them as tall as mountains
Our ant-like brains versus their ramped up artificial intelligence
Our insect-like conduct versus their inter-dimensional travels

We'd make a rather exotic meal, I reckon
They may open a restaurant
Serving living human beings
Like how in China monkey brains were eaten, once
Freshly cracked from their skull

Or perhaps they'd scoop up a whole city
Assuming it's a sort of beehive

They'll study us
Trying to figure out what our vocalizations mean
Trying to figure out why war is so inherent to our species

They'll produce seven-dimensional documentaries
Other beings will stream reality shows featuring
Our executions
Hate crimes
Chemical warfare
The Holocaust

Perhaps it'll be as amusing to them
As how some of us feel
Watching male elks butt heads
Or soldier ants attack a foreign insect
Like young boys blowing up frogs
Or torture pets
Or like when women were accused of witchcraft
And burned alive at the stake (God, that was funny!)

They might set us up against another planet
Simply for their entertainment

My bet is that aliens are gigantic
& if they'd be interested in our resources

They'd probably swallow up the whole planet
En route to more interesting places

We'll end up as ET's excrements
Together with our oceans
Mountains, forests, animals
One huge turd
Gigantic to us
Miniscule to them

We'll be fertilizer floating around in space
Till some other species
Finds & collects us
Use us as manure to enrich
Its intergalactic fields
Produce crops as large as Jupiter

Perhaps this is how humanity will be recorded
At another planet's history books

Commemorating the destruction of our planet
In the universal museum of tolerance

Extraterrestrial kids will learn about us
In excursions to their cosmic museum of natural history

The blue planet will become the brown planet
Like how gorgeous animals
End up cooked, eaten and excreted

Would that be so bad?

THE ALCHEMY OF AMBIGUITY

Ἐν ἀρχῇ ἦν ὁ λόγος, καὶ ὁ λόγος ἦν πρὸς τὸν θεόν, καὶ θεὸς ἦν ὁ λόγος.

i
it's to a symphony of psychotic symptoms that the silicone angels of
ambiguity swing

not out of malice
nor deceit
but implored by desire to embellish
the unadorned word painted by fear

i've seen sacred drag queens
whirl in ecstasy
appearing as hyper-feminine druids with balls

priestesses of kitsch

orbiting a chaotic choreography of freudian slips

& as if they'd speak in tongues

their anatomies turned into consonants
their spirits into *diphthongs*
their erotic shenanigans into vowels

are you listening to yourself?
i can't hear you. what did you just say?
i didn't say anything. you must have heard something i imagined
i think you asked a question; to which i said:

"in principio erat verbum
            et verbum erat apud deum et deus erat verbum."

ii
forgetting is an art i think you said (did i?) as dissimilar as two
parallel questions
as incompatible as carbon & as incompatible as carbon and φλογιστόν,
as merciless as an
electoral college

the word is god
& gods are always prone to mishearing:

i've been told they'll say they said (did they?) exactly what you told me:

which is a warehouse of bought statements

borrowed decibels
in process of building up your words & my words:

consume here the relentless factories of words
word-machines
sentences as
elliptical as guitar-strings squeezed around the neck
prone to supernatural mishearing:

> *the word is a living spirit-being all verdant greening*
> *the word is all creativity*
> *yet shrewd*

iii
this inverted *antiphon* summoned
in an underwater mass chanted by machines
exceptionally talented in misperceiving

misunderstood machines

the logos misspoken & misheard
impossible to unhear impossible to unsay:

this is the alchemy of ambiguity

iv
divine blue light speaks

i couldn't hear it. what did it say?

"osteopath of language," it said
"you've been swallowed down the blue-throated one."

& the silicone angles circled once again around a chaotic
choreography of freudian slips

> *the word is a living spirit-being all verdant greening*
> *the word is all creativity*
> *yet shrewd*

are you listening to yourself?

i can't hear you. what did you just say?
i didn't say anything. you must have heard something i imagined did
you ask a question? to which i said: i already answered.
to which you said: "in principio erat verbum."

DONKEY DIVINATION

All female genitals seemed slashed.

Feeling overwhelmed, I escaped to the balcony in the hope of catching a glimpse of the donkey. Instead of seeing the animal, I noticed a young woman's hazy apparition raising her hand and mouthing words at me. A little girl stood next to her, looking down, crying.

**

The donkey missed an ear. As if it were a long hand without fingers, its other ear waved at me.

Such a clever animal, I thought. *This waving ear must be an omen of some kind but of which kind?*

At times the donkey stopped moving. Looking stunned in my direction, it seemed as if it was trying to make eye contact. In return, I got up from my chair and observed the animal with both my eyes bulging out.

"What is it that you want?" I asked and raised my hand, even though I knew it couldn't possibly hear me from that far, let alone understand human speech.

Thinking about it now, the experience appeared revelatory to me as if existence tried telling me that something important was about to happen.

What could it possibly be?

I lit up a cigarette, looked down and reflected. After a minute or so, the donkey caught my attention again. It had attracted more creatures. Two emaciated calves and a near-hairless dog followed it. Now and then, a family of dark-skinned and underfed humans dressed in dirty rags joined in.

Seen from the same balcony but west of my eyeshot, black silhouettes were buying and selling vegetables under a dilapidated flyover.

There was a river running in between the shanty town where the donkey was leading an unknown religious procession and the crumbling down flyover.

Crowds had gathered at both shores. Industrial-looking crematoria fumed at the horizon.

Judging from the amount of smoke they're doing excellent business; I remember feeling embarrassed thinking, *thousands of funerals are in full swing.*

East of my eyeshot, slightly overweight people were jogging in straight lines. Others like them slouched around wearing headphones in what looked like the meticulously manicured compounds of a fenced housing community. Large spotless homes dotted its premises.

I observed the donkey, all its mammalian friends, the family of underfed humans, dark apparitions buying and selling fruit, the joggers, the slackers, crowds congregating at the crematoria, funerals, fumes, and reflected on the possible meanings of the donkey's missing ear waving at me from what reeked like sea of screeching contrasts.

What was its missing ear trying to tell me?
What was its waving ear trying to say to me?
What's the important thing about to happen?

Bewildered, I returned to the living room. To my shock, on my coffee table something looking like a donkey's ear was trembling.

I've always known, of course, that my imagination had an excessive hold on me, still this image seized me, and a boost of adrenaline shot through my body. After standing paralyzed for what seemed like an eternity, I mustered the courage to approach the ear.

From close by it didn't appear like a hand without fingers. It looked rather like a large smiling mouth with lips opening and closing.

The ear-mouth produced dim vocalizations. I turned my own ear in its direction hoping I'd understand what it was trying to tell me. Perhaps I'd learn what the important thing was that was about to happen.

"Something of utmost importance is happening," I said to myself. "I can feel it."

When I heard the ear-mouth murmuring something resembling, "don't open the," the bell rang. It was the mailman. He had a large package for me. Stupefied, I opened it and found tens of tarot decks with weird donkey characters in it and a few books on necromancy.

***

A month later, my apartment was filled with mammals and under-fed humans. All wanted to know what the donkey's waving missing ear tried telling them.

I had opened the box, but I couldn't understand anything of what was written in these books, *silly abracadabra,* I thought. And the many cards? Head nor tail.

A quiet young woman with a hazy charisma sitting between calves and underfed people picked two cards out of the mess I had made of the decks. She held these in both her hands and said something in a language I couldn't understand.

We gazed into each other's eyes for a while. *She looks famil-iar,* I thought.

Again, she mouthed words. I failed to understand even a single syllable. In the meantime, the mammals and underfed humans had turned my apartment into something resembling part garbage belt, part circus, not to mention the smell.

After some time, the mist-like lady frowned, sighed, got up and placed the two cards on my knees. The moment the cards touched my skin, images of two women living in a pastoral environment instantly popped up in my mind's eye, and my own messy apartment evaporated from sight.

The house in which the two ladies lived had a beautiful balcony looking out on a lush and bucolic landscape. A child was running around in the same home, a girl of perhaps seven or eight years old holding a toy of sorts in her hands. Despite the beauty of this scene, the rhythm of my breathing had gotten faster.

Feeling overwhelmed, I escaped to the balcony in the hope of catching another glimpse of the earless donkey. Instead, I saw a young woman's hazy apparition standing on a balcony raising her hands and mouthing words at me. A little girl stood next to her, looking down and crying.

An uncomfortable premonition had been haunting me since early morning. I tried waving at the girl's apparition, warning her, telling her that something important was about to happen even though I didn't know what, and that she shouldn't ever open the door again, but I saw that the mailman had already entered her building.

"Now it's too late," my brain told me, and a near-unbearable sadness settled in my chest.

I decided to lead the procession with five or six of my most loyal mammalian followers and a few underfed humans. All of them had become disciples when I sliced off my ear about a year ago to prove to my girlfriend that I loved her unconditionally.

First, we stopped at the hazy lady's apartment. The mammals who squatted in her home delivered us a slender corpse wrapped in white cotton.

The most pious of my followers broke out in tears. Others stayed within their personal boundaries and sobbed, leaning against the crumbling down wall. As for me, the sadness had exited my chest. The residual feeling I experienced was bland disappointment.

"We missed a great opportunity," I muttered to myself.

When our religious procession arrived at one of many crematoria, there was so much smoke that I almost mistook the human ashes for dark clouds.

"Has the important thing that was about to happen already happened?" I asked my brain.

When the smoke cleared up, the dark silhouette of a one-eared donkey at the other side of the river apprehended me. Seeing the contours of this black faceless animal induced a sudden weakness in my body. My legs felt feeble. For a second or so, I feared I'd faint, yet this strange sensation seemed to have given my gaze wings. It flew across the river and scrutinized the surface of the water. Flying low above the pitch-black waves, my gaze surveyed the decomposing bodies of those whose families didn't have enough money to buy firewood.
All floating bodies were female.

***

Read here my morning routine: I wake up early and walk over to my balcony to catch a breath of fresh air. In spring, the river's turquoise pigments sizzle on the horizon. The landscape vibrates its gorgeous colors.
Sipping from my cup of coffee, I try jotting down my thoughts. My

hope is to remember my nightdreams. So far, I've been rather unsuccessful.

Instead of recalling a dream image or even a foggy apparition, my thoughts wander off to the pastoral environments in the distance, the shepherds and their sheep dogs herding calves.

"Thank God there's this beautiful landscape to comfort me," a part of myself tells me.

One darker-skinned and rather thin shepherd has a donkey as his companion. It's a peculiar animal. Whenever I look at it, it seems as if it's staring in my direction. I feel sorry for the poor thing. It misses an ear. I wonder how a donkey can lose an ear.

Did somebody slice it off? That'd be so cruel.

Or perhaps its missing ear is a sign?

One morning, feeling exceptionally frustrated about not being able to remember dreams, something in me began contemplating the possible meanings of the donkey's missing ear.

Is the waving missing ear existence's attempt to communicate with me?

A few seconds later my girlfriend's shadow emerged on the balcony wearing headphones. She kissed me on the cheek and said: "I'm going out, jogging, I want to lose weight."

"Is she overweight?" I asked myself and watched how her walking away silhouette disappeared in the dark somberness of the hallway.

Our daughter horsed around the living room holding her beloved stuffed donkey in her hands. It missed an ear. Carla, our hairless sheep dog, had bitten it off.

I looked down and contemplated how everything might be interrelated: my balcony, the missing ear, our daughter's one-eared puppet, the river, my jogging girlfriend wearing headphones, the underfed shepherd, the nightdreams I was unable to recall, the human ashes, and I reflected on the possible meanings of the donkey's missing ear waving at me from what smelt like swamp of unrelated connections.

When I looked up again, the one-eared one had already crossed the river. There were low-hanging clouds obscuring its contours. When winds blew away the human ashes and I could see its other horn waving at me, the bell rang.

"Now it's too late," a male voice in my head whispered, "the dark under-fed silhouettes buying and selling beef under a dilapidated flyover have already joined the ferryman."

All floating bodies were female.

NUDITY

This naked brain,
though part of the body is divorced from it.

This bare body,
though part of the brain
exists uniquely
in the nudity of the head.

Even the head,
extant only
in the braininess of the brain.

All brains are bare.

Their bareness smiles & gloats, when I heedlessly try & dress
the headless bodies in which the brain dwells so well.

URBAN LOVE

Frigid cement,
hitting up bricks
pathologically in love.

Emboldened brains of stone,
as expensive as geometric glass,
animated by the architecture of lack:

Isn't this the burden of non-synthetic sex?

ANTI-LAMPS
for adam cornford

i
i'm a floating
compound ghost
of night-crows

i operate
on sleepless
turquoise & trazodone

flocks of unamerican ur-birds
seeking photosynthesis at night,
are after me

"you're our aleph, tau, theta & phi,"
they're cawing flying behind me
"please devour our anti-lamps."

ii
in kindergarten-universities
indigo-leprechauns are sketching
my contours

"the outer edges have to be narrower
than her volume," they say

"she's our phi,
our sexless salamander
in constant anti-copulation

raised
in two unrelated foreign languages
she hatches under haunted glass

confiscate her anti-lamps"

iii
"during the day she's accused
of having white privilege

at dusk
she becomes an admirador of sorrow,
scavenging for moon-hurt &
the opposite of metamorphosis

indigo-leprechauns love this

pawn your anti-lamps"

iv
an inferior race
of famished mental carnivores
agreed to adopt an anti-lamp

selling isolation & turquoise
at dark-blue prices
is their core business

"its hellenic letters
will help us expand,"
they claim

"we're proud of our
 admiradores of human sorrow"

v
in india you cannot
not have a religion

in india you cannot
not have a caste

in india
damnation in the blue hellfire
of identity is eternal

& here's the thing:

indigo-parents
often praise the
turquoise overlords
that enslaved
their barely-blue
ancestors

devour ten bags of spicy anti-lamps

vi
do you believe in spirit-doubles?
well, in last night's dreaming

my blue spirit-double & i
waltzed on gigantic triangles of turquoise

while slinging anti-lamps

vii
barely round circles
tried swallowing up my contours

"back off," an indigo-leprechaun said,

"you're too new to watch triangles & circles
copulate,

your eyes will catch fire."

hearing this
my burning eyeballs instantly
visualized barely round circles

devouring my anti-lamps

viii
it's the 4th of July, &
indigo-leprechauns running kindergarten-universities
haven't stopped visualizing my contours

their heads mutter:

"somebody is sketching you into existence,
somebody is sketching you out of existence"

yet my blue spirit-double & I,
we're still waltzing on enormous
turquoise triangles

slinging anti-lamps at great velocity

ix
swallowed up
my own contours,

i've exited the floating compound
ghost of night-crows

hunting for photosynthesis at night
a sad ur-bird
caught me & said:

"you're my aleph, tau, theta & phi"

but i devoured all its anti-lamps."

indigo-leprechauns love this

FLESH

To end with:
Greetings to all poets, dead or alive.

My dead (standing firmly behind me) perpetually chant my name:
*in ortu sanguinis per peregrinationem casus ade elementa surceperunt
gaudia in te.*

It's the living that can't stop haunting me.
They seem deader than the dead.
The dead feed me.

Do you think this fact has grown as some sort of natural psychic
mutation of the age?

Or maybe it has something to do with being in the mountains?
The wine of my voice?

I've looked inside my body for my soul.
I only found the *Blue-Throated One.*
There was no soul.

A slave of extremes,
I'm both dead and alive.

I have no need to extract the stone of madness.

One can't be crazy enough.
I'm both Eurydice and Orpheus.

Perpetually giving birth,
my body is *schrecklich.*

In fact, "the" body is *schrecklich*.

All bodies are *schrecklich*.

Thinking about this body,
something effervescent
in which good & evil reunite
absorbs me.

I'm a microbe
dwelling on a microbe
orbiting a microbe.

Language is the final frontier.

Yet like birds in need of a branch to land on,
words are in dire need of human flesh.

ACKNOWLEDGMENTS

Grateful acknowledgements must be paid to those magazines, journals, and anthologies in which most poems of this book were first published.

Zoetic Press, Front Cover Painting
Moon & Sun Magazine, Intergalactic Pharmacist
Anvil Tongue Books, A Vampire Called Eurydice
Clockwise Cat, An Unsarcastically Smiling Sky & Growing Old in America as a Woman
Sulfur Surrealist Jungle, Sexless Half-Objects
Trainwreck Press, The Black Hornet's Mind-Tunnel
Al-Khemia Women's Journal, Nudity & Urban Love
(Also translated into Chinese by Prof. Yong Bo Ma)
Philosophical Egg, Donkey Divination
Trilobite, Flesh
The Ocotillo Review, The Alchemy of Ambiguity (original title The Alchemy of Misperception)
Entropy, The φonemic Body (original title Sonic Pisces Swimming in Silicone Skin)
And Blue Will Rise Over Yellow Anthology, Cosmic Cyclops
Ubu, Taste here the Speed of Hir Desire
Poetrybay, Why on 8th Street?
Aerial Archipelago, Metaphysics of A Pink Bedroom & We'Wha's Journey to D.C.
Live Mag!, Anti-Lamps & Avascular Vishnu

GIORGIA PAVLIDOU is a Greek-born American writer who has lived in California, the Benelux and India. She received her MA in Urdu Literature from Lucknow University, India, and her MFA from the Manchester School of Writing, UK. Her work recently appeared or is forthcoming in Caesura, Maintenant Dada Journal, Puerto del Sol, Clockwise Cat, Ocotillo Review, Philosophical Egg, Live Mag!, Al-Khemia Journal, Entropy and Moon & Sun Magazine. Additionally, Trainwreck Press launched her chapbook 'inside the black hornet's mind-tunnel' in 2021, and Anvil Tongue Books her full-length book of poems and paintings, 'Haunted by the Living—Fed by the Dead' in May 2022. Originally trained in psychoanalytic and systemic psychotherapy, Giorgia practiced as a clinician for about ten years.